The Centered School Library

Engaging Every Learner with Library Skills Centers

By Cari S. Young

UpstartBooks

Madison, Wisconsin

To my parents, Ogden and Virginia Spurlin,
with endless thanks for introducing me to the joys of the library

—C. S. Y.

Published by UpstartBooks
4810 Forest Run Road
Madison, WI 53704

1-800-448-4887

© 2011 Demco, Inc.
By Cari S. Young

The paper used in this publication meets the minimum requirements of American National Standard for Information Science — Permanence of Paper for Printed Library Material. ANSI/NISO Z39.48-1992.

Table of Contents

Welcome to *The Centered School Library*

As you opened this book you may have been wondering, "What *is* a library center?"

Like many educational centers, a library center is an area where students work alone or in small groups, independent of continuous instructor supervision, on activities that reinforce or extend the learning initiated during whole-group instruction.

The Centered School Library offers twelve library center ideas that you can easily adapt and implement in your library. Each center is designed to help students practice the important skills that you teach, focuses on clear objectives, and ties to AASL Standards for the 21st-Century Learner. Additionally, this book provides variations on each center, links to whole-group lessons, and picture book literature connections that you may consider including in your library lessons.

Whether you are experienced with library centers or you are just implementing them for the first time, *The Centered School Library* can help you empower your students to be the most enthusiastic and savvy patrons possible. You're going to love the way centers transform your school library—and the way your students learn.

Let's get started!

—Cari S. Young

Successful Centers: Making a Library Great

Why School Library Centers?

I could use terms like "differentiated learning" and "measurable objectives" to explain why I created centers for my school library. In fact, I've sprinkled some of those technical phrases throughout this book. But I'd prefer to share my reasoning with a practical discussion inspired by some of the comments I used to hear before I created centers in my library—and after.

"Your library looks like a classroom!"

When I began creating centers in my school library, I heard this exclamation many times from teachers, parents, and administrators. They sounded so surprised. They looked around the room and saw much more than bookshelves and computers. They also noticed colorful pocket charts, puzzles, papers, crayons, and other student-friendly materials placed throughout the room, inviting students to engage with them.

Yes, my school library *is* a classroom—the largest, best-equipped classroom on campus! It is not simply a book storage facility, or the place where we have faculty meetings and baby showers—it is a working, teaching classroom.

We school librarians must show our school communities that our libraries are indeed a place for standards-based learning—right at the center of the school's mission—and not a quiet place with nice furniture. If it doesn't look like a classroom and act like a classroom, how will the community know? As budgets are slashed, our contribution to student education must be visible at a glance, each and every day, to anyone who walks through our doors.

"What do I do now?"

Before I implemented work stations, I used to shudder when I heard that question, from a student who'd checked out his books in thirty seconds and was ready to do something else. "Sit there and read quietly" was never a great answer; it might work for a couple of minutes, but soon the student was up again, whistling or leaning back in his chair, or somehow taking my attention away from students who still needed my help. I might hear the same question from the student who didn't return her library books and had all of library time with nothing to do. Sure, she could sharpen pencils or straighten chairs, but that didn't really engage her in active learning. But thanks to learning centers . . .

"Just a minute! I'm almost finished!"

. . . is what I hear now from my students when their teacher tells them it's time to line up and return to the classroom. I see children actively engaged in the centers I've created, and they are reluctant to leave. They've had several activities and projects to choose from, and they've selected one that appeals to their learning style and fits their ability level. We call it "differentiated learning," but all my students know is they always find something they want and are able to do.

"I get it!"

One of the challenges of being a librarian is finding time during class visits to assess student learning. We may set goals and work toward objectives, but seldom do we have enough minutes to give formal assessments. Library centers, when coordinated with your instructional objectives, allow you to observe and measure student learning, and, if needed, report on that learning to your stakeholders (parents, administrators, the school board). Even if no one else reviews these data, you become a better educator as you reflect on your teaching and adjust it based on the results you see.

"Tell me more about the kind of books you like to read."

When I have 20 students engaged at work stations throughout the library space, I can completely focus on that stealthy student who keeps grabbing a book at the last minute, just to satisfy his teacher's requirement that he take a chapter book for silent reading time. I have time to give him my undivided attention, listen to him, interview him, and connect him with the book that could get him hooked on reading for life. There's no way I could make this happen if I had 20 other students clamoring for attention. But with the hum of purposeful activity in the background, I can have a good discussion to help this student move one step forward in his career as a reader. Don't you just love this job?

Planning and Implementation

Now that you're convinced of the difference learning centers will make in your school library, you may be wondering how to begin. The number of stations you create will depend on the space you have available, and the next section (see page 8) will cover the physical aspects of setting up learning centers. Here, we will discuss planning and implementation.

Starting Simple

You may begin using centers at any point in the school year. I recommend that at the start, you set up only one center that requires a mini-lesson to introduce it. The other centers should be fairly uncomplicated and self-explanatory. If you have room for four centers, I recommend starting with an independent reading center, a buddy reading center, a puzzle center, and one center that you will introduce with a mini-lesson.

Independent and Buddy Reading Centers

Independent and buddy reading centers are simple to set up, and most students are familiar with how they work because they've seen them in their classrooms. I keep independent and buddy reading centers going off and on throughout the year to ensure that everyone enjoys success with something that is familiar.

Part of the purpose of a center is to display books in a way that entices students to engage with them, and ultimately take them home to read and savor. I allow students to check out books from any center that I have set up. Independent and buddy reading centers immediately provide a space for contemplation or discussion about books.

Puzzle Centers

Another center that I typically set up right at the start and make available throughout the year is a puzzle center. Again, this is a center that doesn't require much explanation and generates a lot of enthusiasm. You can purchase educational puzzles at discount stores, garage sales, and online, giving you a variety to choose from and rotate throughout the year. Some puzzles are related to authors and books; others are maps of our state, country, or world; and some are images of science topics, like the solar system. I display books related to the topic on the table with the puzzle, so that students get to see a variety of biographies, social studies and science books, etc. The puzzle draws them in, and then they become engaged with the reading materials.

Centers with Mini-Lessons

A mini-lesson provides a model and a focus for student activity at the center. You want to show the children exactly what you expect them to do (how to use the materials at the center, what voice level they may use, etc.), and remind them to check the "I Can" sign (see page 7) if they forget what to do.

> **Tip**
>
> Whenever you set up a new center, introduce it with a mini-lesson. This is key to keeping you centers running smoothly!

Begin your mini-lesson with the students gathered around you at the center. For the sake of illustration, let's assume that you've just had a whole-group lesson about fiction being arranged on the shelf in alphabetical order by the author's last name. Now you want to introduce the pocket chart center that will help them explore this concept. Begin by telling them exactly what you expect them to do. Show them the I Can sign, which might look something like the sample on the next page.

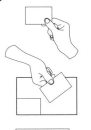

- **I CAN** choose the cards for my grade.

- **I CAN** put the cards in ABC order in the pockets.

- **I CAN** ask a friend or teacher to check my work.

- **I CAN** put the cards back in the zipper bag when I am done.

About "I Can" Signs

A critical component of any library center is a simple instructional sign. Debbie Diller, in her books about setting up classroom centers, calls them I Can signs. I've adopted her language to state center expectations in a positive way. For example, my signs say "**I can** use my whisper voice," instead of "Don't talk loudly." You can laminate these signs or place them in clear acrylic sign holders. Be sure to include graphics for your emergent readers.

After you've given the students their instructions, review the I Can sign and ask two students to role-play the center while the other students observe. You should expect to hear dialogue like this:

Student 1: We're in third grade, so we need to choose the cards from the third grade bag.

Student 2: OK. I've got the bag. Now let's start putting the cards in the pockets.

Student 1: Wait a minute. You put the "B" in the first pocket. We need to leave room for an "A."

The students continue filling the pockets with letter cards. If it takes a long time, you can stop them and allow them to pretend that they have put all of the letter cards into pockets.

Student 1: Now we need to get a friend or teacher to check our work.

Student 2: Let's get a friend!

(Students 1 and 2 select Student 3 from the group.)

Student 3: (Using her best teacher voice) Good job! You have all the cards in ABC order.

Student 1: Now we need to put them back in the bag.

Student 2: OK. I'll hold the bag open while you put them in.

The mini-lesson concludes by having the other students give feedback to the two students who were demonstrating. Encourage as many children as possible to participate by sharing what they observed. They might make comments like: "They put the zipper bag back in the right spot"; "They used their library voices"; or "They took turns."

Thank all of the students for participating. Remind everyone that when they come to this station, they should use the materials in the same way. Repeat the mini-lesson when a class has trouble with a center. It should only take about five minutes.

Management Board

In the classroom, teachers typically use some type of management board to make sure that every student completes every station. As librarians, we typically have hundreds of students because we see and teach every student in the school. I have not found a practical way to maintain a center management system in the library. If you're on a fixed schedule, seeing the same students for a lesson and checkout time every week, you might want to consider creating a system with Velcro, magnets, or clothespins to show the rotation of students from station to station. But because I'm not giving grades—I'm giving additional practice in a variety of skills—I don't feel that it's necessary to exercise this degree of control over who goes to which center.

Reflection Time

To enhance learning, gather students together at the end of their class time and ask them about what they did and what they learned at the work stations today. You can have students talk one at a time, or have them pair-share in quiet voices with the student next to them. Ask them about how they became a better reader, a better information-seeker, or a better problem-solver. This should only take three to five minutes.

If you notice several students commenting about problems at the centers, you may need to make a note to do another mini-lesson the next time this group returns to the library. You don't want bad habits to become routine!

You may also hear comments in these discussions that you want to share on your blog or website, thereby communicating the learning taking place in your library to other members of your school community.

Making Space

Plan Your Space

How you plan your space will play a big part in helping your centers run smoothly. You will want to provide enough room for supplies and activities at each work station, while still allowing traffic to flow around your centers. Here is where the spatial organization side of your brain gets to team up with the creative side.

Tables

First, see how much table space you can use for centers. Do you have tables that can do double duty, serving part-time as a library center and part-time as a student work table? Do you have tables that are primarily decorative, like coffee tables, which could become more functional? Do you have flat, horizontal display spaces that could be used instead for active learning?

Walls

Now, take a look at your walls. (When I say "wall," I mean any vertical space, which could be the side of a bookshelf, study carrel, or file cabinet.) Where do you have wall space without anything in front of it? Look for spaces where a student could stand and touch the wall without having to reach over something else, or where a student could easily see the wall and use a paper and clipboard to respond to what's on the wall.

Floors

Next, look at your floor. What parts of your library sit outside the usual traffic pattern? Where could you place a small area rug to mark the space for a learning center? Look at corners or wide areas where other students could walk around a center if need be.

Finding More Space

Finally, it's time to really get imaginative. Where else could you possibly find space to put a work station? Is there room at the end of a row of bookshelves? Could you move furniture closer together to create a student work area? Are there pieces of furniture in your library that serve no educational function (like an atlas table or an old card catalog) and could either be moved out of the library or converted to a center?

Get Your Number, Fill the Space

Now that you've taken the time to examine your space, what did you come up with? How many centers do you have room for in your library? I keep six centers going at a time in my school library because that number fits my space comfortably, and, if there are four students at each station, an entire class can be engaged in center activities at the same time. With those six areas in mind, I then figure out how I'm going to fill the space using a center planning chart.

On page 9, you'll find an example of a planning chart that shows the centers in my library that I might have around the beginning of the school year. On page 10, there is a blank reproducible planning chart for your own library. In the first column, fill in the locations for centers in your library. Then, make copies of the chart and fill them in with the centers you want to create for the month or week, or however often you choose to change them. (I try to change at least some of my centers every week for variety and to reinforce what I'm teaching in large-group lessons.) The next section provides many ideas for centers that you can build in your library. Browse through them, and be creative! Many can be adapted according to your own space and resources.

Sample Center Planning Chart

Lesson Focus: *Library Orientation*

Location	Center	This Week	Needs Mini-Lesson?
Coffee Table	Word Work	Fiction/nonfiction word sort	
Round table 1 by color printer	Independent Reading	Tables and chairs empty for student readers	
Round table 2 by color printer	Bookmarks	5-finger rule bookmarks for students to color	
3-foot space at end of computer stations	Pocket Chart	Fiction alphabetical order cards	X
Rectangular table	Puzzle Center	I Spy "ABC" puzzle	
Bench by biography section	Read with Someone	Basket with joke books and sunglasses	

Center Planning Chart

Lesson Focus: _____

Location	Center	This Week	Needs Mini-Lesson?

Center 1

—— Independent or Buddy Reading ——

Library and Language Skills Objective: Students will read from a broad range of literary and informational texts with sufficient accuracy and fluency to support comprehension.

AASL Standards for the 21st-Century Learner

3.2.3 Demonstrate teamwork by working productively with others.

4.1.1 Read, view, and listen for pleasure and personal growth.

Grades: K–5

Materials

- A selection of grade-appropriate books
- Chairs and other comfortable seating, such as beanbag chairs
- Special props, such as fun sunglasses
- Stuffed animals
- Laminated I Can sign (printed or handwritten) that features the name of the center and your expectations. *Note: The following sample I Can sign could be used for this particular center, but it should be adapted according to your personal expectations and your library's resources.*

- **I CAN** choose a book from the basket.
- **I CAN** wear a pair of sunglasses from the basket.
- **I CAN** sit next to my buddy.
- **I CAN** take turns reading the book.
- **I CAN** use my Level 1 voice.
- **I CAN** put the book and sunglasses in the basket before I leave.

Set-up

I typically keep both independent and buddy reading centers going all year long. These centers are simple to set up and maintain, and they provide structure to the rather vague direction I used to give students—which was "Sit down and read your book after you've checked it out." A defined work station results in much more "on-task" behavior.

We know that our students may not have books in their homes or even a comfortable spot in their crowded classroom to sit and read. Reading centers give us the opportunity to charm our students with a fun, relaxing environment that encourages them to explore books just a little bit more at every visit.

Buddy Reading Center

For the buddy reading center, I choose a different set of books each week, thinking about what kind of book would be fun to read with a friend. My favorites are joke books, poetry books, magazines, and books especially designed for two voices, such as the You Read to Me, I'll Read to You series from Little, Brown and Company.

Your choice of books can also be coordinated with the focus of your library lessons. For example, if your library lesson relates to poetry, you can include poetry books for two voices in your buddy reading center.

No matter what books you choose, I find that it helps to leave the book covers visible on the table, both to attract students to the center and to let them see an enticing book option that they may not have noticed on the shelf. Include props to add extra fun to the experience. (The older students like to wear fun sunglasses while they read just as much as the kindergartners do!)

You can also allow stuffed animals to live in this center to serve as reading buddies who "listen" to your students read. Children enjoy having such a patient audience, but you will need to demonstrate the difference between a reading buddy and a flying monkey.

Independent Reading Center

If you have a corner of your library available that *seems* secluded but is actually visible to you, that corner will make a great independent reading center. This type of location gives students a spot to feel like they have some privacy. You might use a rug to define the space and pillows or beanbag chairs for comfortable seating.

Typically, an independent reading center simply provides a quiet place for students to read the books they've just checked out. Often, they are excited about their selections and eager to get started. What better place than a relaxing, pleasant, independent reading center? It's a great way for students to pass the time while their classmates are still searching the shelves.

Directions

The instructions for independent and buddy reading centers are simple. I don't require students to be silent in these centers, even for independent reading. Many of our students need to read aloud quietly in order to comprehend the words in the book. And of course, they need to be able to speak aloud when sharing books in the buddy reading center. However, I do require students to stick to a whisper voice, which only the person next to them can hear.

Center Variations

Your reading centers will vary according to the seating area you set up and the books and props you add. In addition, you can change the décor of these centers to match the seasons: a paper fireplace in the winter or a beach umbrella when summer nears. By keeping the expectations and basic set-up (number of chairs, location in the library) the same, you provide the comfort of familiarity. But by changing the decorations, props, and reading selections, you keep student interest high, as they wonder what they will see on their next library visit.

Whole-Group Lessons

When I am introducing students to the joy of reading, I love to share book trailers with them. Book trailers are like movie previews but feature books instead. I project the video images onto the big screen on the wall, and students are enthralled. A school librarian maintains this website with a wide variety of book trailers you can use: booktrailersforall.com.

Literature Connections

Fleischman, Paul. *Joyful Noise: Poems for Two Voices.* HarperCollins, 1988. ISBN 978-0-06-021852-2. (Reading together)

Franco, Betsy. *Messing Around On the Monkey Bars: And Other School Poems for Two Voices.* Candlewick Press, 2009. ISBN 978-0-7636-3174-1. (Reading together)

Hoberman, Mary Ann. *You Read To Me, I'll Read to You: Very Short Scary Tales to Read Together.* Little, Brown and Company, 2007. ISBN 978-0-316-01733-6. (Reading together)

Hoberman, Mary Ann. *You Read To Me, I'll Read to You: Very Short Stories to Read Together.* Little, Brown and Company, 2001. ISBN 978-0-316-36350-1. (Reading together)

Center 2

Alphabetical Order

Library and Language Skills: Students will locate books and information by applying alphabetizing skills.

AASL Standards for the 21st-Century Learner

2.1.2 Organize knowledge so that it is useful.

Grades: K–5

Materials

- Fun foam letters and alphabet poster, puzzles, and/or books (see individual center activity directions for specific details)
- Wikki Stix or pipe cleaners for Wikki Stix activity
- Reproducible game pieces (see page 15) and dice for Alphabet Race activity
- Laminated I Can sign (printed or handwritten) that features the name of the center and your expectations. *Note: The following sample I Can sign could be used for the Alphabet Race activity, but this and I Can signs for all other center activities should be adapted according to your personal expectations and your library's resources.*

- **I CAN** choose an alphabet strip.
- **I CAN** put my car to the left of the A.
- **I CAN** roll a die and move my car forward that many letters.
- **I CAN** say a word that starts with the letter I land on.
- **I CAN** let my friend have a turn.
- **I CAN** keep taking turns until someone goes past Z.
- **I CAN** put the dice and cars back in the tub before I leave.

Set-up (General)

Set up for this center can be as simple as setting out a few appealing alphabet books or as complicated as creating your own alphabetical order puzzle—just be sure to create and display an appropriate I Can list for each activity. Here are several ideas for this center.

Center Variations

ABC Books

Set-up

Preparation for this simple reading center is as easy as A-B-C. Place a selection of ABC books at the study center, both upper level and primary. For example, *A is for Angry: An Animal and Adjective Alphabet* by Sandra Boynton (Workman Publishing, 1987) is a zany, fun book for younger students, but the alphabet series from Sleeping Bear Press has books for all types of older readers with sports alphabets like *T is for Touchdown* and an alphabet for every state, like *B is for Badger.* Jerry Palotta's alphabet books are a combination of colorful illustrations, research, and humor that students enjoy and learn from at the same time.

In addition to providing alphabet books for your students to read and interact with, you can create a personalized ABC book for your own school library. Write a letter of the alphabet on the top of each blank page, and encourage students to add their own entries on the appropriate pages using library terms, titles, authors, your school's mascot, or character qualities emphasized at your school. After this center is finished, put the book in a sturdy plastic cover or comb-binding and make it available as an additional ABC book to read!

Wikki Stix or Pipe Cleaners

Set-up

Place Wikki Stix or pipe cleaners at the center. Both are durable and engaging materials that children can use to form letters. Wikki Stix can adhere to walls or

windows but will not stick to your carpet. Make alphabet books available too, for students to reference as they form their letters.

<u>Directions</u>

Have students shape letters from the Wikki Stix or pipe cleaners and then put them in alphabetical order on a table, window, or wall. Alternatively, the student-made letters can be matched to letters in an alphabet book or on a commercially produced alphabet chart or rug.

The Alphabet Race: An Alphabetical Order Game

<u>Set-up</u>

For the alphabet race, reproduce a set of game pieces from page 15, one for each player. Cut out the road strips and tape them end-to-end in alphabetical order. Put a cup of dice at the center, one die for each player.

<u>Directions</u>

Have students put their alphabet strips in front of them and their game pieces to the left of the A. Players take turns rolling their die and moving that number of spaces forward on the alphabet strip. As each player lands on a letter, she must say a library word (or a book title, character, author, etc.) that starts with the letter she has landed on. If she can't think of a word, she must move back to her last spot. The first player to reach or pass Z is the winner.

Alphabet Connect-the-Dot

<u>Set-up</u>

Provide printed connect-the-dot activities in which the dots must be connected in alphabetical order to create the picture. You can find some of these at bogglesworldesl.com/connect-dots.html. Laminate the activities and let students use wet erase pens to follow alphabetical order and complete the picture (I find that wet erase markers clean more completely from lamination than dry erase markers).

Alphabet Sequencing Puzzles

<u>Set-up</u>

You will probably want to have more than one puzzle at this station so that each student at the learning center has an individual puzzle to complete.

Purchase puzzles on which each piece has a letter of the alphabet and part of a picture. When the letters are put in alphabetical order, the picture is revealed. Each piece of the puzzle is a strip, rather than a traditional puzzle piece.

Alternatively, you could make a puzzle of your own by taking a picture, such as a seasonal photo from a magazine or a printed photo of a scene from your school, and writing the letters of the alphabet in order across the bottom of the page in landscape orientation. Laminate the picture, then cut it into 26 strips.

Whole-Group Lessons

There are many kinesthetic ways to help reinforce alphabetical order. For example, each student can find the fiction shelf labeled with the same letter that is the first letter of the student's last name. Students can line up in alphabetical order by their last names or by author's last names on an index card you've prepared for them.

Literature Connections

Czejak, Jeff. *A Call for a New Alphabet*. Charlesbridge. 2011. ISBN 978-1-58089-228-5. (Alphabetical order)

Kontis, Alethea. *Alpha Oops! The Day Z Went First*. Candlewick Press. 2006. ISBN 978-0-7636-2728-7. (Alphabetical order)

A – B – C – D – E – F – G – H – I

J – K – L – M – N – O – P – Q – R

S – T – U – V – W – X – Y – Z

Center 3

Pocket Chart Learning

Library and Language Arts Objective: Students will use ordering skills (such as alphabetical order and/or the Dewey Decimal system) to better understand the shelving systems in your library.

AASL Standards for the 21st-Century Learner

2.1.2 Organize knowledge so that it is useful.

Grades: K–5

Materials

- Pocket chart on stand or easel. *Note: If you don't have a pocket chart handy, you can easily make one by gluing clear plastic pockets (such as CD sleeves or even plastic baggies) in a grid on a solid piece of poster board, or tacking them to a bulletin board.*

- Spine label cards for sorting (see sample reproducible spine label cards on pages 18–21)

- Pointers (optional, just for fun)

- Storage bags or bins for spine label cards

- Laminated I Can sign (printed or handwritten) that features the name of the center and your expectations. *Note: The following sample I Can sign could be used for this particular center, but it should be adapted according to your personal expectations and your library's resources.*

> - **I CAN** choose the cards for my grade.
> - **I CAN** put the cards in ABC order in the pockets.
> - **I CAN** ask a friend or teacher to check my work.
> - **I CAN** put the cards back in the zipper bag when I'm done.

Set-up

Of course, the key element of this center is the pocket chart. The typical pocket chart attaches securely to a wall, bulletin board, or metal frame at a height that allows every student to reach every row. However, if you would prefer to use a tabletop for this center, desktop pocket charts are available, or your pocket chart may be placed on an easel. (I've even seen charts with pockets large enough for a book, which would allow you to do a book sort at this center.) Choose the set-up that best fits your library space.

You'll want to have different card sets for each grade. For example, kindergarten students should only be expected to sort the letters of the alphabet into alphabetical order. You might use ready-made flash cards or cut up a commercially produced alphabet chart to save time. On the other hand, fifth graders should be able to alphabetize to the third letter, using cards like the examples provided on pages 18–21. (Simply reproduce the pages, and cut out and laminate the cards.) You will also want different card sets for the different areas of your library, such as non-fiction or biography.

To keep the center organized, store the cards in zipper-close bags or bins near the pocket chart.

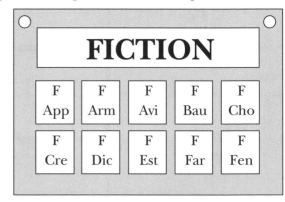

Directions

Note: The following are directions for a fiction pocket chart exercise, but the instructions can be adapted to any set of cards you choose to use.

Your library classes have been studying fiction. They understand that fiction is a work of the author's imagination, and they are eager to learn how to find their own fiction books on the shelves.

- Gather students around the pocket chart. Show them a few fiction books. Point out that the spine label includes the letter "F" for fiction and the first three letters of the author's last name (or explain whichever labeling system you use in your library). Explain that alphabetical order helps us find the books we want to read in the library and that we will be practicing alphabetical order (sometimes called "ABC order" for the younger grades) with this pocket chart.

- If desired, put an "M" card into the chart first, to mark the middle of the alphabet. Then, make the lesson interactive by asking one student at a time to walk up to the chart and put the card you hand her into the correct alphabetical order. To add extra pizzazz, you can have students draw a card from a specially decorated bag or box. Ask the rest of the class to confirm whether or not the student chose the correct spot for the letter, and, if it is in the wrong spot, to correct the card placement.

- Continue until all of the cards have been placed in the chart. This not only teaches alphabetical order, but also illustrates the way we must look to the next row (or library shelf) down to continue the sequence. As the cards are placed, you can model the way that cards may need to be adjusted to allow more room. For example if a student places the "K" right next to the "M," eventually you will need to make space for an "L."

- Explain to the students that this center will be available for two students to take turns placing cards into the correct order. They will need to find the bag (or bin) with their grade level on it, and use only those cards. When they have put all of the cards in order, they should ask you or a library helper to check their work, and then place the cards back into the correct bag or bin.

Center Variations

Again, you can create spine label cards for biography, nonfiction, or any other shelving category in your library. Demonstrate this center whenever you are teaching about a particular category or reading selections from that category. This pocket chart center allows your students to get hands-on experience with correct shelf order—without getting the library shelves mixed up.

- You might also set out materials for students to create spine label cards for this station, using books they like as models, or using their own last name as the author name. They will have a higher level of ownership in cards they have created themselves. You can then have separate, labeled, zipper-close bags for each class so that they can sort their own creations.

- You can also design cards for your state's book award by cutting up a poster with the colorful book covers. Place each cover photo on an index card labeled with the author's last name and laminate them for durability. Students will be seeing the books on the award list as they sort on the pocket chart.

- Instead of sequencing the cards in alphabetical order, you could also use the pocket chart for matching activities, such as:
  - matching a book cover to a spine label
  - matching a book cover to a genre
  - matching a book cover to either fiction or nonfiction

If it is impractical for you or a library helper to check the students' work, you can allow the students to self-check if you prepare an answer key and back it with colorful construction paper. That way, even from a distance, you can make sure that the answer key is facedown on the table as the students are working.

Whole-Group Lesson

Introduce the pocket chart center with an alphabetical order lesson, several of which can be found in the lesson plans of Hanover County Public Schools at hcps2.hanover.k12.va.us/instruction/media/First%20combined%20062003.pdf.

Literature Connections

Bruel, Nick. *Poor Puppy*. Roaring Brook Press, 2007. ISBN 978-1-59643-270-3. (Alphabetical order)

Czekaj, Jeff. *A Call for a New Alphabet*. Charlesbridge, 2011. ISBN978-1-58089-228-5. (Alphabetical order)

Freeman, Don. *A Pocket for Corduroy*. Viking, 1978. ISBN 978-0-670-56172-8. (Pockets)

Kontis, Alethea. *Alpha Oops!: The Day Z Went First*. Candlewick Press, 2006. ISBN 0763627283. (Alphabetical order)

Stinson, Kathy. *A Pocket Can Have A Treasure In It*. Amick Press, 2008. ISBN 978-1-55451-126-6. (Pockets)

Fiction

F App	F Arm	F Avi
F Bau	F Cho	F Cre
F Dic	F Est	F Far

F	F	F
Fen	Gai	Gan
F	F	F
Gif	Hal	Hen
F	F	F
Hol	Ibb	Jac

F	F	F
Kad	Kon	Law
F	F	F
Lev	Lor	Mar
F	F	F
Mye	Nay	Oco

F Osb	F Par	F Per
F Ryl	F Sac	F Sch
F Spi	F Tol	F Tur
F Whi	F Woo	F Yep

Center 4

Book Cart Book Sort

Library and Language Arts Objective: Students will use ordering skills (such as alphabetical order and/or the Dewey Decimal system) to better understand the shelving systems in your library.

AASL Standards for the 21st-Century Learner

2.1.2 Organize knowledge so that it is useful.

Grades: 2–5

Materials

- Shelving cart
- Library books with spine labels
- Shelf markers
- Laminated I Can sign (printed or handwritten) that features the name of the center and your expectations. *Note: The following sample I Can sign could be used for this particular center, but it should be adapted according to your personal expectations and your library's resources.*

- **I CAN** choose a book from the bottom shelf of the cart.
- **I CAN** put that book on the top shelf.
- **I CAN** choose another book from the bottom shelf.
- **I CAN** look at the letters on the bottom of the spine label.
- **I CAN** put the book in ABC order, before or after the first book on the top shelf.
- **I CAN** take turns with a friend, putting books in ABC order on the top shelf.
- **I CAN** ask the librarian to check my work.

Set-up

This may be the easiest center to set up. Simply find a book cart that you are not currently using for shelving or a project. Place several books on the lower shelf in random order (the number of books that you select may vary depending on student age and ability), and leave the top shelf empty for students to work on. If the books that you select for this exercise don't fill the entire shelf, you might want to place a bookend on the cart so that the books don't fall over.

Directions

I like to coordinate this center with the part of the collection that my current instruction is focused on. Generally, this includes the Everybody section, fiction, nonfiction, or autobiography.

- During whole-group instruction, give an overview of how the section is organized, and provide specific examples. Then, allow a group of students to visit this center, where they will take the books that you have placed on the lower shelf, and put them in the correct order on the top shelf.

- Adjust the level of difficulty according to the grade level that you are teaching. For example, if I were having second graders put fiction books in order, I would have each author's name start with a different letter so that they are alphabetizing only the first letter. The older and more capable the students, the more books I would include whose authors' names start with the same letter, to create more of a challenge.

- Can students check out books from this cart? Of course! One of the benefits of this center is that it puts whichever books YOU choose into students' hands. They can look at the covers, flip through the pages, and thoroughly examine the books as they work with them. This is a great way to get overlooked books into circulation.

Center Variations

- This center can also be used to practice using shelf markers. Think of it as a set of training wheels for your inexperienced book grabbers: If they get the books on the cart mixed up, it's not a big deal. Let them learn and practice here, before you turn them loose in the library.

- Use the cart to demonstrate how a bookend works. Do your students leave the books at the end of the shelf in a tumbled mess? Maybe no one has ever showed them how a bookend works. For students who don't have many books in their home, this is a distinct possibility. Explain to them that the books need to be standing up, spines facing you, with the bookend scooted up right next to them. Demonstrate and then let them practice while you supervise. Now you have trained helpers!

Whole-Group Lesson

Introduce this center with a lesson on alphabetical order in the library, like the one from Modesto City Schools at www.monet.k12.ca.us/curriculum/library lessons/Lessons/1st/1_Whats_the_Order.pdf.

Literature Connections

Child, Lauren. *But Excuse Me That Is My Book*. Dial Books for Young Readers. 2005. ISBN 978-0-8037-3096-0. (Finding favorite books at the library)

Fraser, Mary Ann. *I. Q. Goes to the Library*. Walker & Co., 2005. ISBN 978-0-8027-7727-0. (Organization of the library)

Lies, Brian. *Bats at the Library*. Houghton Mifflin, 2008. ISBN 978-0-618-99923-1. (Finding favorite books at the library)

Terry, Sonya. *"L" is for Library*. UpstartBooks, 2006. ISBN 978-1-932146-44-8. (Alphabetical tour of the library)

Center 5

Book Reviews

Library and Language Arts Objective: Students will read independently and produce evidence of their reading. Students will paraphrase what the reading was about.

AASL Standards for the 21st-Century Learner

1.3.4 Contribute to the exchange of ideas with and beyond the learning community.

4.1.8 Use creative and artistic formats to express personal learning.

Grades: 1–5

Materials

- Seasonal shape cut-outs or blank 4" x 6" index cards

- Reproducible book review patterns (pages 26–27)

- Pencils

- Crayons, markers, or colored pencils

- Scissors

- Glue sticks

- Laminated I Can sign (printed or handwritten) that features the name of the center and your expectations. *Note: The following sample I Can sign could be used for this particular center, but it should be adapted according to your personal expectations and your library's resources.*

- **I CAN** think of a book that I love.

- **I CAN** write the title on the heart paper.

- **I CAN** write 3 things I love about the book.

- **I CAN** decorate the heart and give it to my librarian.

Set-up

Designate a table or flat work surface as the location for this center. There, place the I Can sign with the center directions; the supplies listed above; and index cards, shapes, or book review patterns, depending on the Book Review Center you select from the Directions section below.

Directions

These are instructions for some of my favorite centers that encourage students to review library books.

- **Seasonal Book Reviews.** Get students excited about what their peers are reading—and enhance the overall décor and colorful atmosphere of the library—by having students write book reviews on seasonal shapes or index cards. A reproducible heart-shaped book review pattern can be found on page 26, but you can make patterns in any shape you choose. Students should write their reviews and then color and embellish the shape.

- **Copycat Book Reviews.** Copying is absolutely, positively wrong, right? Well, we do allow students to quote directly, provided that they properly cite their sources. The Copycat Book Review Center permits students to copy a blurb from a book they've read onto a review form (see sample on page 27), which they then decorate.

  While this center does not produce a student's original thoughts about a book, it does allow those who might not otherwise attempt a book review to be successful. They practice correct spelling and punctuation, and they get a sense of how people talk about books. Ultimately, their decorative, well-worded teaser for the book is displayed for all to see. Best of all, these students can gradually be moved on to more creative forms of expression as they grow comfortable with the process.

Center Variations

- **Shelf Talkers**. There is an independent bookstore in Austin, Texas, called Book People, that features "shelf talkers" written by store employees. The shelf talkers are typically decorated to resemble the book cover and may include three-dimensional elements, like a torn paper mosaic, or a character from the book. Rather than a formal book review, the shelf talker usually has a few hints or teasers, or an intriguing question to pique the customer's interest in the book. The shelf talker is taped to the shelf in front of the book and provides a colorful, intriguing display.

  Your students, too, can make shelf talkers for the books they love in your library! First, make your own shelf talker as a model. Leave it at the Shelf Talker center work area with the I Can sign that you create and the craft supplies listed in the materials section (for shelf talkers, index cards work well). When my students complete their shelf talkers, I laminate them and use clear tape to adhere them vertically to the edge of the shelf, so they hang down in front of the book they are referencing.

- **Electronic Book Reviews.** If you have a book review component included with your library circulation system, you may already know what a great tool this is to start student book conversations. I have found that students really enjoy writing online reviews, and the system typically allows the reviews to be forwarded to the librarian for approval before they are published for all the world to see.

Designate one of the computers in your library as the book review center so that it is available for students who may not have home access to a computer. This can also be a great team exercise with classroom teachers, who can give students an online review as a writing or reading accountability assignment (and it could be completed using a classroom computer). The library gains more reviews, and the student enjoys a non-traditional assignment.

If you don't have a review component built into your circulation system, start a blog for student book reviews. Make sure that all posts are sent to you as the moderator before they are published. Put a link to this blog on your library webpage and encourage both teachers and students to participate.

Whole-Group Lesson

This lesson plan from Education World provides 25 ways to review or report on a book at www.education-world.com/a_lesson/lesson/lesson109.shtml.

Literature Connection

Auch, Mary Jane. *The Plot Chickens*. Holiday House. 2009. ISBN 978-0-8234-2087-2. (Humorous picture book that touches on publishing and book reviewing)

Title _____

I like this book because _____

_____

_____

_____

_____

_____

_____

_____

_____

_____

_____

Title

By _____

"

_____

_____

_____

_____

_____

_____

_____

"

Source: _____

Center 6

Book Searches and Wish Lists

Library and Language Arts Objective: Students will search the online catalog and use keywords to identify, locate, and access relevant library materials. They will self-select library books for independent reading based on interest and readability.

AASL Standards for the 21st-Century Learner

1.1.8 Demonstrate mastery of technology tools for accessing information and pursuing inquiry.

4.1.2 Read widely and fluently to make connections with self, the world and previous reading.

4.4.1 Identify own areas of interest.

Grades: 2–5

Materials

- OPAC computer station
- Pencils
- Paper
- Reproducible Wish List form from page 30
- Laminated I Can sign (printed or handwritten) that features the name of the center and your expectations. *Note: The following sample I Can sign could be used for this particular center, but it should be adapted according to your personal expectations and your library's resources.*

- **I CAN** think about what kind of book I want to read.
- **I CAN** search on iBistro for that kind of book.
- **I CAN** write what I find on my Library Wish List.
- **I CAN** put my Library Wish List in my library folder.
- **I CAN** use my Library Wish List to find a book on my next visit.

Set-up

Supply pencil and paper near the OPAC computer stations.

Directions

A strong reader usually plans what he will read next. Contrast this ideal to the behavior we may see from less able readers, who walk into the library with little plans or intention. The Book Search and Wish List center can help your students make future reading plans.

You probably already have a lesson that you teach on using your school's online catalog. You show students how to perform effective searches, how to narrow results, and how to sift through the results to find that "just right" book. When you teach this lesson to your class, introduce this learning center, with the expectation that they will use it all year long.

If you are fortunate enough to use Follett's Destiny circulation system, then you have a wish list feature built into your online catalog. If you assign each student a username and password (such as a student ID number), he or she can simply click to add books to an online list at this center. If your circulation system does not have this feature, then students can use pencil and paper to a similar effect. On page 30 you'll find the form I use in my library. My students have a library folder with their barcode glued to the front and protected with a clear label protector. They bring this folder to the library every time they visit, and the barcodes make the checkout process go more quickly. We use the pockets of these folders for our ongoing library projects, like searching for books.

- At your Book Search and Wish List center, students should search for books they want to check out on a later visit to the library if the books are not available (or the student is unable to check out books that day). On their Wish List forms from page 30, students should write down the title of

the book and its location so that on their next visit, they can go straight to that shelf location, even if a computer or the network is not available.

- For stronger searches, create a word wall at this center where you post seasonal or high-interest words so that students can spell them correctly. For example, if you find yourself spelling "dinosaur" or "ghost" over and over, just make a word wall card and put it on the wall in front of the OPAC computers.

Center Variation

- Consider using other technology tools to help your students present their reading interests in a different, more exciting way. For example, a student could use Glogster to create a poster of all of the dog books she would like to read while she is in elementary school. The student could save this project and work on it each time she visits the library. Obviously, the technology tool would need to be taught in a whole-group lesson so that students could work with it individually.

Whole-Group Lessons

You can find ways to use Glogster with your students at edu.glogster.com. A good example of an OPAC search instruction can be found in this lesson plan from Idaho: www.sde.idaho.gov/schoollibraries/docs/lesson/grade3opaclesson.pdf.

Literature Connections

Caple, Kathy. *Duck & Company*. Holiday House, 2007. ISBN 978-0-8234-1993-7. (Duck tries to find the right books for customers at his bookstore.)

Finchler, Judy. *Miss Malarkey Leaves No Reader Behind*. Walker & Co., distributed to the trade by Holtzbrinck Publishers, 2006. ISBN 978-0-8027-8085-0. (Miss Malarkey helps students find books they will love.)

Gerstein, Mordicai. *A Book*. Roaring Brook Press. 2009, ISBN 978-1-59643-251-2. (A young girl who lives in a book searches for her story.)

Name: _____ **Teacher:** _____

My Library Wish List: Books I Want to Read Next

Title	Author	Location

Name: _____ **Teacher:** _____

My Library Wish List: Books I Want to Read Next

Title	Author	Location

Center 7

Genres

Library and Language Arts Objective: Students will read and comprehend literature in a variety of genres.

AASL Standards for the 21st-Century Learner

4.1.3: Respond to literature and creative expressions of ideas in various formats and genres.

4.1.4: Seek information for personal learning in a variety of formats and genres.

Grades: 2–5

Materials

For Genre Voting Center

- Ballots from page 33, ballot box, and privacy divider for genre voting

For "Name that Genre"

- "Name that Genre" game cards and directions from pages 34–40

For Genre Posters

- Poster board, alphabet stencils, and markers for genre posters

For all Genre Center Activities

- Laminated I Can sign (printed or handwritten) that features the name of the center and your expectations. *Note: The following sample I Can sign could be used for the Genre Voting Center activity, but it should be adapted according to your personal expectations and your library's resources.*

- **I CAN** decide what my favorite fiction genre is.
- **I CAN** write my favorite genre on a ballot.
- **I CAN** write my name and grade on the back of the ballot.
- **I CAN** put my ballot in the ballot box.

Set-up (General)

The activities for this center are easiest to complete on a flat surface, like a tabletop. Be sure to create and display an appropriate I Can list for each activity. For further set-up instructions, refer to each activity.

Center Variations

After you've spent time with the entire group teaching genres, set up one (or all) of the genre center activities below to give students further practice exploring genres and thinking about their own reading choices.

Genre Voting Center

This is a good center to set up during genre study or when your community is having an election and you want students to experience the democratic process.

Set-up

- Make copies of the ballots on page 33, one for each of the following genres: Realistic Fiction, Fantasy, Mystery, and Historical Fiction, OR whichever genres you wish to teach/feature in the election.

- On each sheet, write a single genre in each book ballot (so you will have a single sheet of book ballots for Historical Fiction, a sheet of book ballots for Poetry, and so on).

- Reproduce each sheet onto different-colored copy paper, laminate if you wish, and cut out the ballots. Place each set of ballots in a separate container or clear plastic baggie.

- Create a ballot box. (I decorate a shoebox with colored paper, cut a slot on top, add the word "vote" in decorative letters, and use it for various voting opportunities throughout the school year.)

- Create a voting booth using a science fair-type trifold board on top of a table, or use a carrel, if available. Place genre ballots and the ballot box in the booth.

Directions

Have students enter the Genre Voting Center voting booth. There, they should select their favorite genre and put the appropriate ballot in the ballot box. When every class finishes voting, use the colorful book ballots to create a huge pictograph on the wall, about eight feet high, to demonstrate the math conccpt of a pictograph and report the preferences of your students. (In my school, Horror always wins by a landslide.)

"Name that Genre" Game

Set-up

- This is a game for two or more players. Create cards with the title of a book and its description, emphasizing the elements that classify it into a certain genre, and laminate them so that they'll last. Sample cards that cover REALISTIC FICTION, FANTASY, MYSTERY, and HISTORICAL FICTION are provided on pages 34–39.

- Read through the game instructions from page 40 and place them at the center with the game cards. When students are seated, review the instructions with them, if necessary, before they play.

Create a Genre Poster

Set-up

- Provide the craft supplies listed in the materials section at the center for a student or group of students to create a genre poster to display in your library. You'll need poster board, markers, and alphabet stencils for nice lettering.

Directions

- Have students print out book covers on the color printer or draw their own replicas of book covers to illustrate examples of the genre they wish to feature. When they are finished, display their work on library walls or as part of book displays.

Whole-Group Lesson

An elaborate genre study lesson plan is available on ReadWriteThink at www.readwritethink.org/class room-resources/lesson-plans/genre-study-collabora tive-approach-270.html?tab=4#tabs.

Literature Connection

Hopkins, Jackie Mims. *Joe Bright and the Seven Genre Dudes.* UpstartBooks, 2010. ISBN 978-1-60213-051-7. (A fractured fairytale describing genres)

Ballots

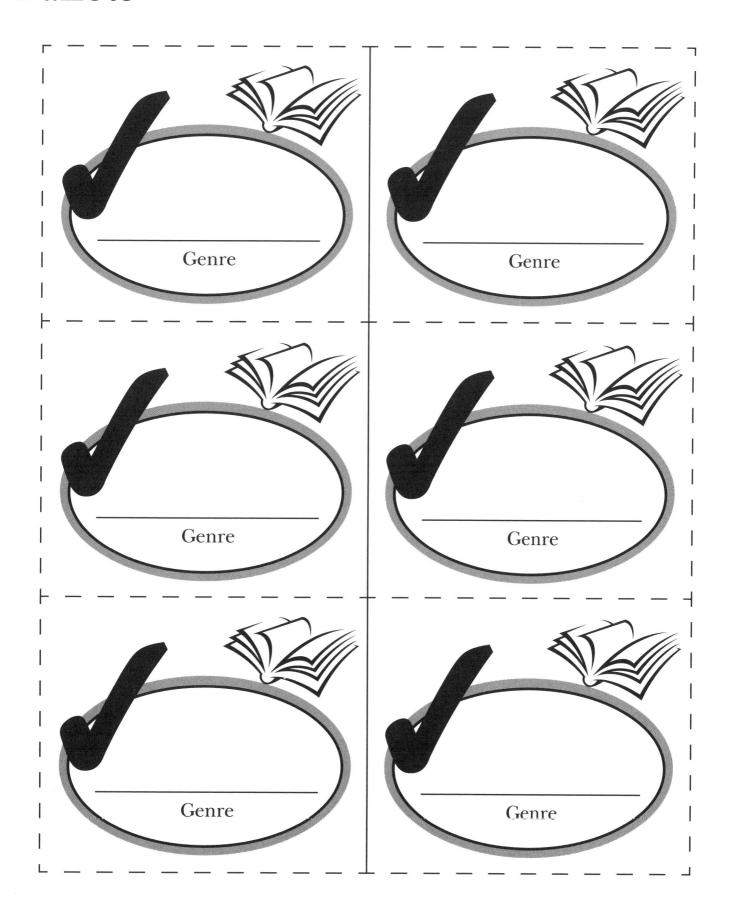

Genre

Genre

Genre

Genre

Genre

Genre

Lost and Found

by Andrew Celements

Twins move to a new school that is only expecting one of them. No one can tell them apart. So they decide to take turns going to school and staying home.

Realistic Fiction

Diary of a Wimpy Kid

by Jeff Kinney

Greg Heffley keeps a journal about funny things that happen at home and school.

Realistic Fiction

Ivy and Bean

by Annie Barrows

Two girls become friends, even though they like different things. They get into mischief in their neighborhood.

Realistic Fiction

Stink and the World's Worst Super-Stinky Sneakers

by Megan McDonald

Stink enters a contest to identify smells at a museum exhibit.

Realistic Fiction

Beezus and Ramona

by Beverly Cleary

Ramona's big sister, Beezus, thinks she is a pest. She ruins the birthday cake and locks a dog in the bathroom.

Realistic Fiction

Henry and Mudge

by Beverly Cleary

Henry's big dog, Mudge, is his best friend. Sometimes Mudge drools and eats things he shouldn't eat.

Realistic Fiction

How to Train Your Dragon

by Cressida Cowell

A timid Viking boy trains a dragon and becomes a hero to his village.

Fantasy

The Spiderwick Chronicles

by Toni DiTerlizzi

Three kids move into a new house and find elves, goblins, and other magical creatures.

Fantasy

The 39 Clues Series

by various authors

Two orphans must travel all over the world as they find 39 clues, solve puzzles, and survive dangers to find a family treasure.

Mystery

Nate the Great and the Halloween Hunt

by Marjorie Weinman Sharmat

Nate discovers his friend's missing cat by finding clues and thinking about them while he eats pancakes.

Mystery

The Case of the Spoiled Rotten Spy

by James Preller

Jigsaw Jones must find the missing prop so they can film a TV show in his town. He must prove that the spoiled star is not the thief.

Mystery

The Dark Stairs

by Betsy Byars

Herculeah Jones helps her mother solve a murder by finding clues in a creepy old house with a dark staircase. When she is in danger, her hair frizzes.

Mystery

Fablehaven

by Brandon Mull

A brother and sister discover a preserve for fairies and imps and other magical creatures.

Fantasy

The Chronicles of Narnia

by C. S. Lewis

In the magical land of Narnia, animals can talk, and a powerful lion battles against an evil queen.

Fantasy

The Sisters Grimm Series

by Michael Buckley

Two sisters live in a magical town filled with fairy tale characters, like giants and magic mirrors.

Fantasy

The Magic Tree House Series

by Mary Pope Osborne

Jack and Annie travel through time to places that they read about in books. They must escape danger and get home.

Fantasy

Hiss Me Deadly

by Bruce Hale

A gecko detective tries to figure out who stole his mother's pearls. A watch, a tiara, and two computers are also stolen from his school.

Mystery

Sammy Keyes and the Hotel Thief

by Wendelin Van Draanen

Sammy Keyes sees a burglar steal something from a hotel room. She must solve the crime before the burglar finds her.

Mystery

Little House on the Prairie

by Laura Ingalls Wilder

In the 1800s, Laura Ingalls travels across the frontier with her family. They live in a log cabin and meet Native Americans.

Historical Fiction

Mr. Tucket

by Gary Paulsen

In 1848, a fourteen-year-old boy is kidnapped by Native Americans, then lives in the wild with a one-armed trapper.

Historical Fiction

Gabriel's Horses

by Alison Hart

During the
Civil War, a slave
raises racehorses for
his master and dreams
of becoming a jockey.

Historical Fiction

The Invention of Hugo Cabret

by Brian Selznick

In a Paris train station in
1931, an orphan boy is
caught stealing parts
to repair a robot.

Historical Fiction

The Courage of Sarah Noble

by Alice Dalgliesh

In 1707, Sarah Noble
must be brave when her
father leaves her with
a Native American family
for several months.

Historical Fiction

The Door in the Wall

by Marguerite De Angeli

In medieval times, a boy
who can't walk cannot be
a knight. But he
still finds a way to
save the castle.

Historical Fiction

Directions for Name that Genre

1. Place all cards facedown in the middle and mix them up.

2. If two players are playing, each player draws 12 cards.
   If three players are playing, each player draws eight cards.
   If four players are playing, each player draws six cards.

3. Players take turns in ABC order by first names. The player whose first name comes first in the alphabet is Player 1.

4. Player 1 turns to the player on his right and reads her the title and description of a book.

5. Player 2 guesses the genre of that book.

6. If Player 2 guesses correctly, she keeps the card and places it on the table in front of her. If Player 2 is wrong, Player 1 keeps the card and places it on the table in front of him.

7. Take turns until all cards have been guessed or the time limit is up.

8. Count the cards in front of each player. Whoever has the most cards is the winner!

GENRES

Mystery: A suspenseful story about a puzzling event that is not solved until the end of the story.

Fantasy: A story with impossible elements, like talking animals or magical powers.

Historical Fiction: A story that happens in the past. The setting is real, but some of the characters are made up from the author's imagination.

Realistic Fiction: A story with imagined characters that could happen in real life right now.

Center 8

Reference Books

Library and Language Skills: Students will use text features in age-appropriate reference works to locate information. They will locate, access and evaluate print and online information sources.

AASL Standards for the 21st-Century Learner

1.1.1 Follow an inquiry-based process in seeking knowledge in curricular subjects, and make the real-world connection for using this process in own life.

1.1.4 Find, evaluate, and select appropriate sources to answer questions.

Grades: 2–5

Materials

- Reference books (see individual center activity directions for specific details)
- Pencils
- Paper slips or forms for center activities (see individual center directions for details)
- Laminated I Can sign (printed or handwritten) that features the name of the center and your expectations. *Note: The following sample I Can sign could be used for the New Words for the Dictionary activity, but this and I Can signs for all other center activities should be adapted according to your personal expectations and your library's resources.*

- **I CAN** think of a brand new word for something.
- **I CAN** write my word on the paper from the basket.
- **I CAN** write the definition of my word (what it means).
- **I CAN** write a sentence to show what my word means.
- **I CAN** put my paper in the Frindle box.
- **I CAN** listen to the morning announcements to see which new words are read aloud.

Set-up (General)

Most of the reference book centers described below require reference books, paper, and a pencil for a response. The books can be stacked on the table or kept in a clear magazine holder at the center to keep things neat and organized. Be sure to create and display an appropriate I Can list for each activity.

Center Variations

The following centers review skills for reference books including the encyclopedia, dictionary, thesaurus, almanac, and atlas. Although we often use online versions for our research projects, we employ many of the same skills required for the print versions—particularly knowing which tool to use! Additionally, you may have a library like mine that does not have enough student computers for an entire class. This center will help students acquire the knowledge they need to effectively use either text or electronic versions of these reference books.

Almanac Answers

Set-up

Have an almanac available at the center for each student. Prepare a container of question slips that feature questions related to weather in your area and in other parts of the world. Place another small container at the center for students' answers.

Directions

Have students select and fill out a slip of questions and put it in the answer container when they are finished. At the end of the week, draw one slip with the correct answers to win a library prize, such as a bookmark, lunch in the library, or a guest spot on the morning announcements.

The slips can ask questions about weather in parts of the world that your students are studying, or parts of the world that have been in the news recently. This activity will help your students to see what information is available in the almanac as they search for the answers. It will also help them to learn about the climate in other places. Here is an example of a question slip:

> ## Find the Answers in the Almanac!
>
> What is the average temperature in January in San Antonio? _____
>
> What is the average temperature in January in Anchorage, Alaska? _____
>
> What is the average temperature in January in Honolulu, Hawaii? _____
>
> Name: _____
>
> Homeroom Teacher: _____

Of course, you can change the questions based on what you want your students to focus on. Instead of weather, you might choose flags or continents.

Which Reference Tool?

For all research projects, it's important to know which reference tool to use. Place an example of each type of reference book on the table. Have a set of cards in one color with the names of the books, and a set in another color with the use for each. For example:

Dictionary	Helps me learn about words. I can find their meanings (definitions), spelling, pronunciation, and parts of speech.
Thesaurus	Gives me options of many words with similar meanings. Helps me find the best word to use.
Encyclopedia	Helps me learn facts about the world around me. I can find out about people, places, things, and events.
Almanac	Helps me find statistics (number facts) about different things that happened in a specific year.
Atlas	Helps me find places. I can find maps of states and countries.

Students should examine the books that you set out as examples, and then match each book with its name card and the card that best describes its purpose. For example,

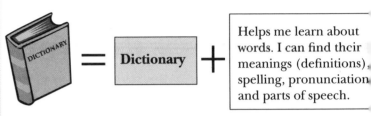

Guide Word Gurus

<u>Set-up</u>

Place several student dictionaries at the center with scratch paper and pencils. If you have a library blog, you can have your students respond electronically.

<u>Directions</u>

Provide a whole-group lesson about using dictionary guide words. Then, allow students to engage with this center.

Instruct students to open the dictionary to any page. This adds a random element to the activity, so make sure they are using a student dictionary to ensure that they don't encounter inappropriate vocabulary.

Once they have opened to a random page, have students look up the definitions of the two guide words they see on the page. On the scratch paper or the blog, instruct them to write one sentence using BOTH of the guide words correctly. See how creative they can be! This is great practice for strengthening both dictionary skills and sentence-writing skills.

New Words for the Dictionary

<u>Set-up</u>

If your students have read *Frindle,* they may already be familiar with the idea of creating a brand-new word for a familiar object. At this center, students will use their imaginations to create a new word, as well as make up a definition for that word. Make dictionaries available at this center, as well as forms for students to complete (see example on page 43).

```
....................................................
:  New Word: _____     :
:                                                :
:  Definition: _____      :
:                                                :
:  _____     :
:                                                :
:  _____     :
:                                                :
:  Sentence that shows the word's meaning:        :
:                                                :
:  _____     :
:                                                :
:  _____     :
:                                                :
:  Name: _____       :
:                                                :
:  Homeroom Teacher: _____      :
....................................................
```

Directions

Direct students to complete the form and share their words and definitions with each other.

Note: If the entire class will be participating in this center, have students drop their definitions into a class bin when they are finished sharing them. When you have a definition from everyone, you can gather the group together and create a class dictionary of created words, with funny guide words and all!

Atlas

Set-up

Put a few atlases on the table for this center, as well as scratch paper and a cup of sharpened pencils.

Directions

Have students look at the atlas and locate a destination related to a topic of your choosing. Choose the locations you want them to look for based on what the students are studying—current events, a state capital, a city in Asia, a city near the equator, or a national park, etc. When they have selected their location, have them write it down on scratch paper and take it to a computer, where they can then find that location on Google Earth.

Thesaurus

Set-up

In this center activity, students focus on themselves and their own names. It's a great way to make students feel special and develop enthusiasm for exploring the thesaurus. For this activity you'll need several baby name books and thesauri, as well as paper and

pencil, unless students are responding via blog or wiki. If you have time, you can design a reproducible slip for students to fill out, or use the example below:

```
....................................................
:  My first name: _____      :
:                                                :
:  According to _____       :
:                                                :
:  (baby book source), my name means _____       :
:                                                :
:  _____     :
:                                                :
:  According to _____ (thesaurus       :
:                                                :
:  source), a synonym for my first name is: _____ :
:                                                :
:  _____     :
....................................................
```

Directions

Have students look up their first names in the baby name book and record their meanings. Then, instruct them to look up the meaning in the thesaurus, and record a synonym for the original word.

Whole-Group Lessons

Education World has good dictionary skills lesson plans at www.educationworld.com/a_lesson/lesson/lesson206.shtml.

Literature Connections

Barrett, Judi. *Cloudy with a Chance of Meatballs*. Atheneum, 1978. 978-0-689-30647-1. (Imaginative weather events)

Coy, John. *Around the World*. Lee & Low Books, 2005. ISBN 978-1-58430-244-5. (A game of basketball played literally around the world)

Clements, Andrew. *Frindle*. Simon & Schuster, 1996. ISBN 978-0-689-80669-8. (Word creation)

George, Lindsay Barrett. *Alfred Digs In*. Greenwillow Books, 2008. ISBN 978-0-06-078760-8. (An aardvark digs through a dictionary, all the way to "Z.")

Shulevitz, Uri. *How I Learned Geography*. Farrar, Straus and Giroux, 2008. ISBN 978-0-374-33499-4. (A refugee boy studies a map to escape the hunger and misery of daily life.)

Center 9

Word Study

Library and Language Skills: Differentiate between fiction and nonfiction books. Interpret words and phrases as they are used in a text.

Grades: K–5

AASL Standards for the 21st-Century Learner

3.1.3 Use writing and speaking skills to communicate new understandings effectively.

Materials

For Word Sorts

- Magnetic surface, magnetic letters, and words written on cards backed with magnetic tape, such as the examples on on pages 46–50

For Making Words

- Magnetic letters, letter tiles, or letter cards
- Timing device (egg timer or minute timer)
- Dictionary
- Magnetic letters for making words
- Letter cards for making words
- Commercial or educational word games
- Word games from the newspapers
- Wet erase markers
- Blank paper or card stock
- Crayons, colored pencils, or markers
- Letter stencils
- Laminated I Can sign (printed or handwritten) that features the name of the center and your expectations. *Note: The following sample I Can sign could be used for the Word Sorts Center activity, but this and I Can signs for all other center activities should be adapted according to your personal expectations and your library's resources.*

- **I CAN** put the words Fiction and Nonfiction next to each other on the table.
- **I CAN** look at a book card.
- **I CAN** put the card under the word "Fiction" if I think it is fiction.
- **I CAN** put the card under the word "Nonfiction" if I think it is nonfiction.
- **I CAN** sort the book cards into a "Fiction" stack and a "Nonfiction" stack.
- **I CAN** ask a friend or the librarian to check my work.
- **I CAN** put all of the cards back in the basket before I leave.

Directions (General)

This is another center that can be coordinated with whatever library lessons you are teaching students at the time. Word study tasks will focus on the vocabulary (including phonics and spelling) for the content area and should be differentiated by grade level. Be sure to create and display an appropriate I Can list for each activity.

Note: If you are in a typical elementary library, which may have kindergarten (or younger) students through fifth grade, you'll need to differentiate at this work station because of the variety of reading levels. You can use labeled bins or shoe boxes for the activities for different grades. When you introduce the center, you can explain this feature to students as you instruct them on the importance of putting materials away in the proper place before leaving.

Center Variations

Word Sorts

A word sort involves the categorization of individual words written on cards. Many word sort books are commercially available and emphasize spelling and vocabulary skills. For this particular activity, you'll need a tabletop or magnetic surface so that the cards can be arranged in columns beneath the category names.

Set-up

For this "word sort" center, think of two or more categories related to a topic you are focused on in your general library skills instruction, and then think of items that can be sorted according to the categories. For example, the reproducible cards on pages 46–50 can be sorted according to categories of FICTION and NONFICTION. Reproduce these cards and back them with magentic tape if you wish, or create your own according to what you are teaching. For instance, you might create cards for a note-taking word sort in which students sort phrases according to TRASH or TREASURE based on a research question. Or you might create cards that have questions on them that can be sorted by RED-LIGHT versus GREEN-LIGHT (closed versus open-ended). No matter what you decide to use as text for the cards, be sure to create an answer key.

Directions

Place the word sort cards at the study center and have children sort them on a magnetic surface or tabletop.

Making Words

Another activity that I like to include in this center is a game of making words from other words.

Set-up

Print and laminate a fairly long word that you have introduced in a lesson, such as "autobiography" or "classification." Place it at the study center along with a timer; a dictionary; and magnetic letters, letter cards, or letter tiles.

Directions

Instruct students to see how many words they can make out of the letters of the laminated word, using magnetic letters, letter cards, or letter tiles. Explain that they can use the dictionary to check their spelling. Add an egg timer or minute-timer for an additional competitive challenge to this activity. Alternatively, have students write down their list and give a prize at the end of the week to whomever had the longest list of words spelled correctly.

Word Games

Set-up

For an easy-to-set-up word study center, include a word game purchased at a toy store such as Boggle or Scrabble, or from an educational publisher, such as Highsmith's "What's the Word" game (for library terms).

You could also laminate word study games from the newspaper and provide wet erase markers for the students to use. This allows students not only to interact with words, but it also introduces them to a feature of newspapers, which not all students have in their homes. Rotate different games throughout the year.

Word Bookmarks

Set-up

Fill a jar or basket with words related to your direct instruction. For example, if you are teaching genres and concentrating on mysteries, you could include words like sleuth, clue, detective, mystery, crime, fingerprints, genre, book, read, puzzle, solve, investigate, and so forth.

At the study center, provide the basket of words, pieces of paper or card stock that have been cut into four lengthwise pieces (approximately two inches by eleven inches), colored pencils, markers, crayons, and lettering stencils. Students can write the words on the paper and then color or illustrate it to create their own bookmark. If possible, have one of your imaginative students create an excellent sample for you to post with the I Can list that you create for this center.

Whole-Group Lessons

Scholastic has a lesson in which you pair up students to explore difference between fiction and nonfiction books, and create a chart of their findings. This can be done as a whole-group lesson. Visit www2.scholastic.com/browse/lessonplan.jsp?id=435.

Literature Connections

Schotter, Roni. *The Boy Who Loved Words*. Schwartz & Wade, 2006. ISBN 978-0-3758-3601-5. (A magical appreciation of words)

Fiction

Nonfiction

The Frog Princess

The Life Cycle of a Frog

Owls in the Family

All about Owls

Gregory the Terrible Eater

Eating Right

Diary of a Spider

Insects and Spiders

Goldilocks and the Three Bears

Bear Cubs

Click! Clack! Moo! Cows that Type

Life on a Cattle Farm

The Day Jimmy's Boa Ate the Wash

Amazing Snakes!

Scaredy Squirrel at the Beach

Busy, Busy Squirrels

Don't Let the Pigeon Drive the Bus!

Pigeons

The Talking Nest

A Nestful of Eggs

The Nature of Lions

Library Lion

The Show-and-Tell Lion

Center 10

Listening and Recording

Library and Language Skills Objective: **Library and Language Skills Objective:** Students will integrate and evaluate information presented orally.

AASL Standards for the 21st-Century Learner

1.1.6 Read, view, and listen for information presented in any format (e.g., textual, visual, media, digital) in order to make inferences and gather meaning.

Grades: K–5

Materials

- Cassette or CD player with multiple headphone jacks, or multiple Walkman-type cassette or CD players or multiple MP3 players
- Headphones
- Several copies of each book with accompanying cassette tapes or CDs
- Laminated I Can sign (printed or handwritten) that features the name of the center and your expectations. *Note: The following sample I Can sign could be used for this particular center, but it should be adapted according to your personal expectations and your library's resources.*

- **I CAN** get a book from the box.
- **I CAN** put on the headphones.
- **I CAN** press Play.
- **I CAN** listen to the story.
- **I CAN** press Stop.
- **I CAN** put the books back in the box.

Set-up

This center allows a few children to sit in a quiet spot and listen to an audio recording of a story. As they listen, they hold the book in their hands and turn the page when they hear the cue.

Initially, I did not think that my students would enjoy this older technology, given all the colorful electronic book options we have available online, but I quickly found them smiling as they pressed the buttons on the tape player and turned the pages of their books. It's almost like having another adult in the room with you, reading to your students with expression and fluency. Students can relax and enjoy the experience, without having to worry about decoding the words.

This is a fairly easy center to set up and maintain; I keep mine up for most of the year and change out the books and recordings based on the seasonal topic or library instructional focus. You can use commercially produced recordings, or you can make the recordings yourself to add more variety. If you make them yourself, consider including newspaper and magazine articles, too. You can also ask older students to create recordings (see Center Variations) that match library books in your collection.

If you are putting a single-cassette or CD player with multiple headphones at this center, you will want the player to remain in a central location, either in the middle of a table or, if space is tight, on top of a plastic container with the books and CDs/tapes stored inside. (Otherwise, clear magazine files are great for keeping books at this center, as they allow the covers to be visible, and they keep things neat and easy to put away.)

If you are using individual cassette/CD/MP3 players, the materials need to be returned to a central location, but the students can find any comfortable, quiet spot in the library for listening. Consider using stickers to label your listening devices' directional buttons if they are difficult to decipher. I put colored smiley face stickers on the buttons that students will need to press so that pre-readers learn, for example, that the green smiley face means "Play."

The book at the listening center may be a title just for fun, or it can be related to library instruction. For example, in February near Presidents' Day or when you are discussing biographies, you could place David Adler's *A Picture Book of George Washington* (Holiday House, 1990) in this center. When you are teaching lessons about poetry or the solar system, put Douglas Florian's *Comets, Stars, the Moon and Mars* (Harcourt, 2007) here for your students to discover. You may have several titles at this center at once if you have individual cassette/CD/MP3 players.

If you want a written assessment of student learning at this center, you can include a response form for the student to complete as (or after) she listens. This can be a direction to draw the picture she sees in her mind as she listens, or it might be a graphic organizer, or it might be a request to respond to a prompt specific to the title. Alternatively, you can have students who listened to the same book retell the story or discuss it with each other after listening. Or, they can make a prediction based on the book cover, then discuss their prediction at the end.

Directions

Before turning students loose with their books and audio devices, give them a brief overview or reminder of how the audio players work, and remind them of any other ground rules you have for this center. Then, they are free to listen and read.

Center Variations

On occasion, consider turning the listening center into a recording center. Allow students to make their own tapes or digital voice recordings of books that they enjoy reading. Provide a bell or some type of sound cue for students to use to signal the listener that it's time to turn the page. Alternatively, you could have a listening and a recording center set up at the same time as the Listening Center, if you have enough space and equipment.

Whole-Group Lesson

Hear a story about listening at the Screen Actors Guild Storyline site at www.storylineonline.net. Select "Knots on a Counting Rope." Discuss the ways that listening was important for the characters in the story.

Literature Connections

Sayre, April Pulley. *Dig, Wait, Listen: A Desert Toad's Tale.* Greenwillow Books, 2001. ISBN 978-0-688-16614-4. (A spadefoot toad listens for rain.)

Schaefer, Carole Lexa. *The Biggest Soap.* Farrar, Straus and Giroux, 2004. ISBN 978-0374306908. (A young boy listens to the stories of his South Pacific island community.)

Center 11

Newspapers and Newsletters

Library and Language Skills Objective: Students will write narratives about real experiences or events and use technology to produce and publish their writing.

AASL Standards for the 21st-Century Learner

3.3.4 Create products that apply to authentic, real-world contexts.

3.3.5 Contribute to the exchange of ideas within and beyond the learning community.

Grades: 2–5

Materials

- Dictionary
- Thesaurus
- Examples of newspapers or newsletters
- Special pens, such as colorful or glittery gel pens
- Letter trays filled with different types of paper
- Computers
- Laminated I Can sign (printed or handwritten) that features the name of the center and your expectations. *Note: The following sample I Can sign could be used for this particular center, but it should be adapted according to your personal expectations and your library's resources.*

- **I CAN** look at one of the Ugly Duckling books in the box.
- **I CAN** think of three good things about an Ugly Duckling book.
- **I CAN** write three sentences on an index card.
- **I CAN** draw a picture about the book on the index card.
- **I CAN** write my name and teacher on the back of the card.
- **I CAN** give the card to my librarian.

Set-up

In this center, students will create content for a school newspaper. Depending on the computer availability in your library, you can either set up this center at computer stations or on a tabletop with writing materials. If they write on paper, consider having a newspaper class or club that meets separately to either copy the handwritten articles or type them into a program like Microsoft Word or Publisher. Or you can have students write blog entries in a school-safe environment like Edublogs and copy selected entries into your newspaper publishing program.

One thing that I have found helpful is to decide upon a focus for the newspaper ahead of time so that students have a solid starting point. For example, you might give them a theme of winter sports, which could include reviews of books related to winter sports; student stories about winter sports they've participated in; an explanation of clothing and equipment used in winter sports; articles about favorite basketball teams, skiers, or skaters; and tales of winter Olympic athletes. Or you might choose to focus on a particular type of writing: expository, persuasive, or descriptive, or you might simply provide a writing prompt (like "my favorite pet") and choose a variety of responses to publish.

Time is always a consideration for library centers, and this one is no exception—especially as some students may wish to research before writing. Make sure that they have an opportunity to finish up their articles, either by making the center available at some other time, or by imposing a word limit.

Directions

- Explain to students that at this center, they will be creating a newspaper. It will not be graded—it will be published for a real audience to learn from and enjoy. Show them examples of newspapers or newsletters.

- Depending on whether students are working at computers or by hand, explain the software or the craft and writing materials.

- Give students the topic or starting point that you have decided on, and have them take a minute or two to decide on a name for their publication.

- Explain that they will have to work together to decide who will write each article, and how they want their publication to look.

- When students have finished their articles, collect their handwritten work or printouts, and make copies to hand out to other students and teachers.

Center Variations

If your school already has an official school newspaper, you can create a library newsletter by displaying books at the center that you want students to write about. You might choose new arrivals, seasonal titles, curriculum connections, or ugly ducklings that deserve a second chance. Your library newsletter can be published electronically as a blog, displayed in the library, or printed and delivered to teachers for classroom use.

Another topic for library newsletters can be author profiles. Students can view an author's website and write an article to encourage other students to read books by that author. You can help teach information literacy skills in mini-lessons during the writing process.

Even when I'm not teaching a writing lesson in the library, I try to provide both an encouraging and an instructional comment for each piece of writing that a student hands to me. I want to help move them just a little bit forward in their skills. For example, I'll say, "I love the way you used adjectives to describe your puppy. Now, what do you need to add to the end of this sentence?" This and other writing centers will provide you with the opportunity for on-the-spot writing instruction.

Whole-Group Lesson

ReadWriteThink has a great lesson plan about creating classroom newspapers at www.readwritethink.org/classroom-resources/lesson-plans/creating-classroom-newspaper-249.html.

Literature Connections

Downard, Barry. *The Race of the Century*. Simon & Schuster, 2008. ISBN 978-1-41692-509-5. (News media cover the race between the tortoise and the hare.)

Sandin, Joan. *Coyote School News*. Henry Holt & Company, 2003. ISBN 978-0-8050-6558-9. (Students in a one-room school house produce a school newspaper.)

Center 12

Making Inquiries

Library and Language Skills Objective: Students will conduct short as well as more substantial research projects based on focused questions. They will demonstrate an understanding of the subject under investigation.

AASL Standards for the 21st-Century Learner

1.1.3 Develop and refine a range of questions to frame the search for new understanding.

Grades: 1–5

Materials:

- Colorful markers
- Index cards, sticky notes, or butcher paper
- A container to collect responses
- Laminated I Can sign (printed or handwritten) that features the name of the center and your expectations. *Note: The following sample I Can sign could be used for this particular center, but it should be adapted according to your personal expectations and your library's resources.*

> - **I CAN** write a question about school on butcher paper.
> - **I CAN** write my name and teacher's name under my question.
> - **I CAN** put my marker back in the box.

Set-up

We want to encourage discovery and inquiry in our school libraries. Sometimes it seems like we're so busy filling our students with knowledge that we forget to take time to explore with them, to consider the questions they wonder about on their own. This center allows students to express their curiosity, and it encourages them to find answers to their questions—or the questions of their peers. After all, we spend our time teaching students to read well and to be skilled library users so that they can find and evaluate information for the rest of their lives.

The inquiry center is really the culmination of the other library centers outlined in this book. The simplest way to set up this center is to place a length of butcher paper across a table, put a container of markers on top, and make an "I Can" sign with the directions. You may choose to write a guiding topic across the top of the paper such as, "Things I Wonder about School."

Directions

This center needs two sparks to really get it going. First, it must be introduced to the whole group, and second, you must break down the "blank paper barrier" by writing a few questions of your own on the butcher paper. I've found that students who tend to follow directions very closely can be intimidated by an open-ended question and a blank piece of paper, and your handiwork can serve as a nice ice-breaker.

Once you've written a couple of questions of your own on the paper, students have an example to follow. They know that it's fine to write in different directions, to write on paper without lines, to write something that may seem like a silly question to other people. They see that you've written your name under your question, modeling that expectation for them.

After your paper is filled with student questions, display it on the wall of a nearby hall, where everyone can see the curiosity that you encourage in your library space. Feature one of the questions as a "Wonder of the Week" on your webpage or morning announcements, and encourage students to search for an answer. Interview the first student to give you the correct answer, and share the interview with the school. Discuss how the student came to that answer. Was it via the Internet?

A reference book? A personal interview? How did the student determine that the source was credible?

Center Variations

- Supply index cards or sticky notes for your students to write their questions on, and then attach those to a bulletin board or length of butcher paper. Questions written on colorful paper with a variety of markers make a vibrant, eye-catching display of curiosity!

- Instead of opening up a "Wonder of the Week" question to the entire school, choose a Wonder of the Week for an individual class. Have students in that class spend their library time answering the question once you have finished whole-group instruction. For example, suppose the open-ended topic you supplied was, "Things I Wonder about Famous People." A question in this category might best be answered with an online subscription database. After you've introduced the database in a whole-group lesson, choose a student question for other students to answer by using that database. In all likelihood, students will be more motivated to find the latest pop star's birthday instead of George Washington's. When student questions are being answered, the research methods being employed to answer them suddenly become a lot more interesting and generate a lot more enthusiasm.

- Create an I Can sign for finding the answer to the "Wonder of the Week." Provide pencils or pens and slips of paper for students to write down their answer to the question and the source where they found the answer. I don't require a full, formal citation for this, but I do want to reinforce the principle of acknowledging the information source. Have students place their

answers in a container. When you review these, you have data about the level of mastery for this skill. Additionally, you can encourage future participation by drawing from the correct answers and awarding a bookmark or other library prize.

Whole-Group Lesson

You can find a lesson plan about generating questions and finding answers using nonfiction texts at www.readwritethink.org/classroom-resources/lesson-plans/adventures-nonfiction-guided-inquiry-183.html.

Literature Connections

McDonnell, Patrick. *Me—Jane*. Little, Brown and Company, 2011. ISBN 978-0-316-04546-9 (A young Jane Goodall wonders about the natural world.)

Pfister, Marcus. *Questions, Questions*. NorthSouth, 2011. ISBN 978-0-7358-4000-3. (Rhyming questions about nature)

Taylor, Barbara. *I Wonder Why Zippers Have Teeth and Other Questions about Inventions*. Kingfisher, 2003. ISBN 978-0-329-56993-8. (Questions and answers)

Ready, Set, Go! Resources for Success

Now you've read about all kinds of ideas for centers in your school library, enough to last you through the entire school year. But if the prospect of so many centers seems overwhelming to you now, just set up one. The enthusiastic response you receive from your campus will encourage you and give you the energy to get the next center started.

Once you get rolling, you're sure to get even more ideas for library centers everywhere you go: at librarian conferences, in classrooms, even at discount stores and garage sales! Please share them at www.library-centers.com. I'd like for us to be able to help each other, so that no library is left behind in the era of quiet, dusty spaces where students and teachers feared to tread. Pay it forward, share your bright ideas, and make school libraries a better place for ALL of our students!

Resources and Websites

Supplies for your centers:

- Upstart has games and puzzles related to library skills, perfect for use in your centers: www.high smith.com/upstart.

- Another source of games and supplies for your centers is the Really Good Stuff catalog: www.real lygoodstuff.com.

- Scholastic has books with reproducible card games inside them, like *40 Sensational Sight Word Games,* and *Vocabulary-Building Card Games,* all available at www. Scholastic.com. You can copy and laminate these card games to use in your centers.

Online Library Lesson Plans

I find great whole-group library lesson plans on these websites:

- elementarylibraryroutines.wikispaces.com/Home

- www.hisdlibraryservices.org/Scope_and_Sequence/scope_and_sequence.htm

- www.sldirectory.com/libsf/resf/libplans.html

- www.highsmith.com/librarysparks/pages/magazine-index

- www.readwritethink.org

Bibliography

Portions of the Library and Language Standards are drawn from the Common Core Standards, available online at corestandards.org, © 2010. National Governors Association Center for Best Practices and Council of Chief State School Officers. All rights reserved.

AASL Standards for the 21st-Century Learner are available online at www.ala.org/ala/mgrps/divs/aasl/guidelinesandstandards/learningstandards/standards.cfm and are copyrighted by the American Association of School Librarians, a division of the American Library Association.

Each of the following books influenced me and my ideas as I implemented centers in my school library:

- *Literacy Centers in Photographs* by Nikki Campo-Stallone. Scholastic, 2008.

- *Literacy Work Stations: Making Centers Work* by Debbie Diller. Stenhouse Publishers, 2003.

- *A Place for Wonder: Reading and Writing and Nonfiction in the Primary Grades* by Georgia Heard and Jennifer McDonough. Stenhouse Publishers, 2009.

- *Practice with Purpose: Literacy Work Stations for Grades 3-6* by Debbie Diller. Stenhouse Publishers, 2005.

- *Spaces and Places: Designing Classrooms for Literacy* by Debbie Diller. Stenhouse Publishers, 2008.